WHEN LOVE CHANGES EVERYTHING

Poems of Love and Longing

Iris Mede

ISBN-13: 9798779088893
ISBN-10: 1477123456

Cover design by: Art Painter
Library of Congress Control Number: 2018675309
Printed in the United States of America

"I want to be the air that inhabits you for a moment only. I would like to be that unnoticed and that necessary."

--MARGARET ATWOOD

CONTENTS

PREFACE

This is a collection of poetry written during the beginnings of a relationship. Is there a more romantic time in one's life. Is there a more exquisite experience than the first few steps along the journey of love and passion? Once Cupid's arrow has hit, all we want is to escape the ordinary and enjoy the romantic, passionate moments when high desires soar and the visions of love become vibrant. So gather your lover close and discover yet again how beautiful and sublime new love can be in these poignant love poems.

TWO SUNSETS

I send your way two sunsets,
As my gift to you;
One I snatched from a perfect day,
With a perfect hue.

The second was the brightest,
Because it featured stars,
That seemed to spin around the spot,
Where Venus visits Mars.

You may have these sunsets,
Straight from my memory;
No one else has these scenes,
Save only you and me.

THE HAND

Your hand that hovers over me,
Knows not what it may take;
I am a field of flowers:
Gather blooms, do not hesitate!

A MIRROR

You weren't sure, so you asked a mirror,
About your love for me;
The mirror spoke and answered back,
Our love was meant to be.

You acted on that sentiment,
And rushed to me that day;
And never knew that I had bribed,
The mirror on precisely what to say!

YOUR MIND

Your mind is sharp, like a razor's edge,
and shaped to be on your own;
Get ready to share your life.
In a while, you won't be alone

IT IS HOW

It is how your mind thinks sometimes
that makes me love you so,
Like a tree, knurled and unconstricted,
with virtue that proudly grows.

A LOVING SEA

I knew that you,
Thought of me today;
I felt it so, even though
You were so very far away.

I sensed your love,
Rise and sweep over me
As the shore feels caressed
When it's kissed by a loving sea.

YOUR LOOK

I love the way

you look at me
way across a room,
as we share a glance
--as our eyes do dance
to our own tune of love.

I could put my hands up
to feel the love come to me
coming straight across at me
-oh, how soft as it touches me
oh, how warm your love for me.

YOUR PRESENCE

Your presence follows me,
Through the day everywhere;
No mere apparition,
You are the spirit
And the soul that I share.

Though you dwell every day,
In your own body too,
I feel you in me,
Reciting to my heart
All day long, "I love you."

A WIND

A wind is blowing through my mind,
And strikes me in my eyes;
It hums and sings and tells me things,
And attempts to make me wise.

The wind has whispered where I must go,
And all the things that I must do,
I know the wind is truthful,
For I know the wind is you!

DROP OF RAIN

"Nothing is perfect," sighed the fox.

-- Antoine De Saint-Exupery, "The Little Prince"

From a single drop of rain,
that falls upon your heart,
you run and head for cover,
lest the drop was just the start.

But life is not perfect, orderly,
or can ever be complete;
We cannot expect that from life,
or in anyone we meet.

Love is like that also:
It's never tailored to our needs.
As if you can find someone faultless,
with happiness guaranteed.

Seek the most important:
Just what you need.
Then concede the rest,
that's how you'll succeed.

THERE EXISTS

There exists someone else,
Who looks a lot like me;
Another one whose life is poor
Someone I shall never be.

Her hair is dull and flat,
And yet is like my own;
Her eyes are like my eyes,
But no life in them is shown.

Her body is a useless thing,
Hungry for love that never came;
Her soul is frozen in the dark,
Not warmed by love's fine flame.

I saw her in the mirror once,
And she looked a lot like me;
But love has spared me from,
The one I shall never be.

I KNEW

I knew, from that moment on,
I knew that we would be together.
It was as clear as if I had read it
in a history book:
The US declared independence in 1776;
You and I would meet and fall in love.
It was that sure and certain to me.

When was that exact moment?
I don't recall it precisely,
but I know it occurred
while we were eating pasta
at an Italian restaurant.
You had just said something
about why you had responded to my ad
--something about loneliness
-- and I took your hand and thanked you
for making that call.
I then promised you, silently,
that neither you nor I would ever be lonely
--ever again.
We then made plans to take a day trip.

You brought out paper and carefully wrote
your full name and your work number:
I was to call you,

if I couldn't make the trip.

Driving home that evening
I had your note clutched in my hand
as if it were a medal
I had just been awarded.
I lifted it high
and felt struck by its weight:
It felt as if I was holding
all my future and all my happiness
in my hand.

The moon was bright that evening
and all the streets seemed to shimmer.
Later I transferred your work number
to my telephone book and tore up the paper
you had written your number on into bits
and let them fall casually into my wastebasket.
I couldn't let anyone else know
how much those bits of paper meant to me

HOW CAN I

How can I sleep
with sounds outside my window
Call and recall your name.
Every creature there knows
all your fall routine.

HUNGRY

My heart grows hungry every December
for Christmas like it never was.

Is it that way with you?
Can it be that way with you?

For there is a place somewhere,
with people gathered there,
smiling and laughing,
happy and singing,
and surrounded by a scene
that looks just like the scene
of the happy ending
in Dickens' "A Christmas Carol."

Don't you think that way sometimes too?
Don't you think it can come true?
Can it be with you?

DREAMS

If some dreams reoccur,
let me mark the one,
that I intend to have always,
like a classic film rerun.

I will not change a thing,
it is a perfect dream;
I just need to change my nights,
to make my days supreme.

ANCIENT TROY

She often sits alone in the woods,
Where she goes, and she broods;
For she is dismayed,
With the woeful world, she sees.

She was born too late,
And much too great,
To be content,
With dismal times like these.

Her beauty is beyond belief,
But she cannot find relief;
In these times,
Or in the future that she foresees.

She was born ever to yearn,
For ancient times to return,
Like fabled Troy,
Or her life with Hercules.

I THOUGHT OF YOU

I thought of you as I walked,
In the dimming of the day,
In a place where people rushed,
Their humanity their way.

I thought about how you live your life,
In a way that is your own,
So different from the rest,
Like noise is from a poem

YOU

The following poem I write
Will be solemn and serious,
I promised myself.

Then you entered my mind,
With your sensual eyes,
And your stirring lips,
And made a witty, irreverent,
Immodest remark.

All the seriousness left,
And my mind thought of you;
Only you alone.
And you are never
Solemn and serious.

A STUPENDOUS SKY

This sand-bank --the backbone of the Cape --rose directly from the beach to the height of a hundred feet or more . . . by as steep a slope as sand could lie on . . . . It was like the escarped rampart of an ancient fortress . . . with the view of an autumnal landscape of extraordinary brilliancy, a sort of Promised Land . . . under a stupendous sky.
--Henry David Thoreau, Cape Cod

I want to stand next to you
When you see a stupendous sky;
And I want to stand by you
When you need someone close by.

I want to be there always
For all reasons throughout the year;
I want to hear you whisper things
That only I will hear.

I want to have you always
Close your eyes on me and sleep;
I want to always hold your hand
And always have your love to keep.

TRAVEL

We all travel
on this road of life;
Some of us disheveled
and some of us with strife.

I travel now
with you, my friend,
as my lover and my muse.
Tired am I of journeys,
without perfect views.

ONE WISH

I have one wish, my love,
if I should die today;
Take my ashes to the sea
on a windy day in May.

There, on a sandy hilltop,
when seagulls fill the sky,
throw my ashes to the breeze,
and whisper your good-bye:

"For you have loved me more
than any I have known;
And you have been the best,
that life to me has shown!"

On that day in May,
on that same hilltop,
think of me that day,
But don't think I'm not with you,
Or that I've ever gone away.

I would never be gone,
if I exist in your memory,
And if your memory goes on,
with you, I will be!

"For you have loved me more

than anyone I have known;
And you have been the best,
that life to me has shown!"

YOUR LIFE

I came to your life,
You didn't know me;
I had such humble offerings,
So what were you to gain?
Did I presume too much,
or ask too much?
It wasn't easy, you know,
To see you in such pain.

I shouldn't have done that:
Questioned you so much,
But I had my reasons,
Even if they seemed too vain.
You were so pressure-packed
Coiled just like a spring,
And I was not to blame.

You seemed so lovely,
And so lonely,
I wanted to comfort you;
When I did, you saw the need,
That I, too, just like you,
Needed a friend like you.

I TASTE YOU

I taste you as a liquor,
That was brewed in oaken vats,
Made from trees that grew,
In primeval habitats.

Inebriated of you I am.
And debauched of you as well;
My mind seems to reel and feel,
As if my tankard held a magic spell.

YOUR LOOK

I love the way you look at me
across a room,
as we share a glance
--as our eyes romance
dancing a special dance
to our own tune of love.

I could put my hand up
and feel your love,
coming straight across at me
--oh, how soft as it touches me
oh, how warm your love for me.

MY LOVE

My love, my darling, my dear:

This morning my heart is full

and bursting with emotion and passion.

We were together for three whole days!

Three days that were filled with experiences,

encounters, and memories that will last a lifetime.

Just now, I miss your hand in mine and your face,

your lovely, lovely face so much it becomes painful.

I try to salve my heart by remembering experiences

of the last few days: walking hand in hand through

tiny streets, wandering through uncommon shops

with you, exploring life's little pleasures with you.

I remember it all so well. But, oh, how I miss you!

I miss your face and your sweet glances.

I miss how I would wake up each morning

and see the morning sun filtering through

the lace curtains and how it would touch your face

with a warm glow. I miss how each morning

we'd wake up, and I would ask you: "How are you?

Did you sleep well?"

Oh, my love, I do so long for you this morning!

I feel I never tell you enough how I think about you

and how much I love you. I also don't think

that I'm even nice enough to you. My love,

how I'd like to hold you and cover you with kisses

-- happy, joyful kisses and tell you how glad

I am when I am with you!

My mind is crowded this morning with

the warmest, heart-rending memories you gave me.

From all sides, they come to me: How delightful

the weather was, how the sun was dazzling

and intense, how charming that place was

where we stayed where people could be heard

through the late hours of the night,

strolling in groups, laughing, while we made love.

It was altogether one of the tenderest three days of peace

and happiness I could dream of.

Thank you for the last few days.

Thank you!

Thank you!

Thank you!

YOUR HEART

I can feel your heart
stirring at last
from its long,
love-avoiding sleep.
The glacier you built
in which it's kept
is melting, exposing
the love within so deep.

I NEED TO

As you know, I need to touch you,
As needful as a flower needs the rain.
Touching you brings me satisfaction,
And a kind of ever-lasting pain.

Let me touch you on the face and mouth,
And the place where you want privacy.
I promise I'll share myself as well,
And let your touch form a bond with me.

AN INSTANT

Just for an instant in the expanse of time,
We share this moment,
--our moment,
And only you and I can make it more,
--fully much more than just wasting time.

To see your beauty,
To touch your face,
To live this moment within love's grace,
Will make this moment stretch out,
To a bright tomorrow,
Filled with love that doesn't pain,
Or ever sorrow.

Come to me now,
My living dream and my life's desire,
Fill my heart with joy and feed my raging fire;
Stay with me always, within my heart,
Joined together now, never to ever part.

I WANT

I want us to know each other
as much as and as well as
we think we know ourselves.
The "we" we show the world
is not good enough a pearl.

Your feelings and your thoughts
must be as sure to me
as my very own.

I want to know all your cries
and what each signifies.

Climbing in your mind and down,
all around, inside of you
is what I want to do.

I want to travel through parts so new
that you have not charted them before.

That is what I want to do.

AS WE WALKED

As we walked together slowly,
Beside a languid lake nearby,
Hand in hand like lovers,
The friendly night
erased the angry day
And filled the grateful sky.

You and I talked together
Of a dozens things or more,
And each word seemed newly heard,
As if always
they had been waiting,
Along that same lake shore.

The amber moon glimmered,
Above the water's glow,
And the waves sent back their raves,
As discretely and so sweetly,
They shimmered,
To tell the moon hello.

The sky was busy pouring
It's blackness all around,
And night bird's sounds abound,
As they practice
Soaring

For one last go around.

I looked at you with all the love,
That I have kept inside of me,
All the passion that's been imprisoned,
And which you,
My dear, my love,
You have set it free!

WHAT SHALL I SAY

What shall I say in this poem?
What words do I choose this time?
This grows more difficult day after day,
While love grows easier at the same time.

There are only so many words,
To be arranged in only so many ways;
No wonder I get complaints from tired verbs,
That get winded from appearing in multiple schemes.

Yet all I can do is hope and trust,
That you will glean some sense and thrust,
But also try to enjoy my arrangements of sounds,
That come to you solely to proclaim this love profound.

MY HOMETOWN

I've wandered far from my hometown,
Going back, they wouldn't know me now:
Walking in and having you by my side,
They would look at you and ask me how.
When I go back to my hometown,
I'll look those people straight in the eyes;
The one they thought would never go far,
Turned out to be the one who got the prize!

THERE ARE MANY

There are many exotic places
I would like to take you to.
One of them is Macao.
There, on a nearby hillside,
is an ancient Buddhist garden,
that is always wrapped in clouds

To get there, you must climb,
up picturesque stairs and pathways,
that seems endless and very high.
And sometimes rain,
a warm, drenching rain,
makes it seem like Mt. Sinai.

It takes two hours
to reach that place
that seems halfway to the sun.
But there is no place
with more quiet peace,
except perhaps Shanghai-la.

MY DREAM OF YOU

My dream of you had me worried.
I sat down and
tried talking to it,
but it wouldn't speak to me.
I asked if there was anything wrong,
but it said no.

I left it alone for a while,
but it didn't change.
It seemed more distant then,
and more melancholy.

I offered to take it for a walk
or to a movie, but it said no.
It just grew more sullen and withdrawn
and was not breathing well.

It started to look wane and withered
and I became concerned.
So, in desperation, I took it forcefully
out into the evening air,
and forced it to feel.

It began breathing normally again
and the worst was over.
I saw it this morning:
It looked great!

I SAW YOU

I saw you
and every dream
I've ever dreamed
was looking back at me;

Every longing of my life
seemed to be fulfilled.

Cynicism just disappeared,
and caution deserted me
like it was never there.
And I couldn't care.

What you brought
was absolute serenity.

I wanted you,
like a child all alone
seeking safety;
and finding it with you.

I exulted in the sun,
knowing I had won.
--the impossible dream to me,
that somehow came to be!

YOUR SMILE

Existing on your smile
each day
I know that I am saved
and privileged beyond
words and thanks.

On this troubled planet
each day
troubled people dart about
while I glide along with you
and your smile.

Far off in the heavens
each night
God-made stars and planets
are scattered in the sky
for only you and me.

Away from your smile for even
just a day,
and I don't exist.
Nothing seems real or even false.
Life exists where there is only us.
I don't have reason or cause
each day
to live except for you.

IRIS MEDE

I have stopped my life
except for life I live with you.

IF I STARE

If I stare long enough
I can see the future:
A bright day
that awaits me there
in some future time,
in some future way,
on a path
I have not yet taken,
but will,
and where my
woes are forsaken.

SOMETIMES

Sometimes when I touch you,
It feels like I am touching my other half.

That's how close and comfortable,
touching you feels to me.

And when I hold you in my arms,
It is like I've found a home after being lost.

I am at long last home with you.
I feel I will never be alone anymore.

We have finally found each other
and have been joined together... again?

That is the way it feels, as if our love
is deja vu, and is not really new.

We touch like the sea touches the shore:
surely, completely and fervently.

MY DARLING MUSE

My darling muse,
sweet one that inspires me,
you have filled my mind
with intrepid thought
while I've lain my head
upon your breast
and heard you whisper
all that you have taught.

Go to the rise,
and I will follow you;
inspire me with ardor,
and with innocence
that still reside
deep inside of you;
I will guide my star
by the light of what you are
and what heartens you.

SO MANY TIMES

So many times a day
I want to take you in my arms
and hug you and kiss you
and tell you that I love you.

I want you to know that I love you,
and that I love you so very much;
You no doubt know that by now,
but I want to tell you that
over and over and over again.
For the telling of my love for you
is a pleasure to me.

And every day also I want to tell you
how beautiful you are,
and how wonderful I feel
when I look at you.

Oh, I long to kiss you
and look into your eyes
and tell you of the love
that wells up in me and overflows.

It is also a pleasure to hear you
say that you love me,
without hesitation now,
without embarrassment now

and without restraint or reserve.

Know that your love will be returned,
over and over and over again
and that I'll never stop telling you
that I love you,
and that I'll never stop wanting you
to say to me that you love me.

A LETTER TO A BELOVED HUSBAND

This is a paraphrase of a moving letter from a bereaved wife to her husband that was written after his death at the Battle of Gettysburg. He was just a private, not an officer or a general, and she was just an ordinary woman, albeit with uncommon emotion.

My husband has been taken by God, but I will always keep his memory. I could never forget him, my husband: He was the best man that ever lived, at least that is what I thought. Maybe it was just that I got exactly the right kind of man for me.

We were married for over 18 years and they were hard years at that. Many things were done without, for the sake of the future and for the children. We had 11 children. If I had it to do over again I would live the same life again. I could not ask for more. Just when we were beginning to stand on our feet he went off to war and I lost him. I can't get over it. When I think of him now I remember how happy he was in the morning of each day. Just before he went off to work each day he would tell me that he would hurry home to me. When he went off to war he also told me he would hurry home to me. But, I have been waiting for a long time now and he will never come home to me again.

THE TIME

The time for love has come for you,
and don't you think it is due?

Though you thought it might never come,
finally it is here, slightly overdue.

ONCE WE WALKED

Once we walked in the rain,
several blocks.

That could have been a lot,
had you not,
turned to me and smiled,
and made those drops,
taste like pink champagne.

I COULD TELL

I could tell
that I was climbing
when I first met you
and my feet
suddenly left the ground.

The feeling was
somewhat alarming
as I stumbled
and struggled
to find safe level ground.
The light was poor
and I wasn't quite sure
where the feelings
of clammy hands
and cowering fear
came from
--or if they would ever stop.

But, no,
they have never stopped.

AN ANGEL

When we kissed the first time,
We became the project of a new angel,
Who needed us to fall in love to let her get her wings.

Now we've fallen in love --and how,
So our new angel will indeed get her wings,
And she also gets a special merit badge that says:

"To Honor the Unique Duty of
An Angel Who Helped Create
A Very Special Sort of Love."

I WANT TO SAY

I want to say, "I love you,"
without words,
but in everything I do;
And I want to hear
your reply
in the same way too.

Your face, your beautiful face,
could take a decade
to quiet compliment;
soft silent kisses, I will leave
as my gestures
to mark your resplendent.

IT IS OUR TIME

It is our time to play,
After the day's work is done;
Take my hand and join me,
Just you, me, and the setting sun.

All that our hearts forgo,
All that never seemed to come,
Shall be ours to savor as a minor favor,
From our friend, the setting sun.

LOST

Lost in love's passionate embrace,
I see your lovely, loving face,
And my soul wants to take your soul
      and
        fly
High above the highest clouds
In the crimson sky,
Never to return to earth.

ABOUT THE AUTHOR

Iris Mede

She is an indie author and editor from West Hollywood, California. In 2002, she began publishing poetry under different pseudonyms for the Los Angeles Easy Reader.